60 THINGS TO DO WHEN TURNING 60 YEARS OLD

By Elaine Benton

Bridge Press

support@bridgepress.org

Please consider writing a review!

Just visit: purplelink.org/review

ISBN: 978-1-955149-25-9

TABLE OF CONTENTS

INTRODUCTION

Your 60th birthday is coming up, and with it is a chance for you to take charge of your life. Getting older brings certain advantages that just aren't available to the younger set, including the ability to do things without worrying what other people think. So, view your 60th year as the one where you start thinking about the life you've always wanted and get busy making it happen by adding joy, being practical, improving yourself, reconsidering your career, leaving a legacy, and adding spice.

1

ADD JOY

Aging is not a bad thing, especially because by the time you get to 60 years old, you know a lot about what you like and don't like. You know which activities bring you joy and which ones you'd rather skip. You might discover that you have time on your hands that was once filled with kids' school events or sporting contests, along with shuttling them back and forth. It's time for you to fill your days with the things that make you happy.

2

TRAVEL

The idea that people want to travel when they get older and retire is a little bit cliché, but there's a good reason for its popularity. Travel is one of the activities people report brings them the most joy. Whether they're traveling to see family and friends or simply to new sights, many people enjoy getting away from their everyday lives, even just for a few days. You don't even have to travel very far to get the benefits of satisfying your wanderlust.

As you turn 60, some fantastic travel ideas include going on a cruise, renting a house on the beach, recreating your honeymoon (or going on a second one that's even better), and planning an annual trip with your adult kids and/or grandchildren. Visiting other countries is also recommended when you are older because you can better appreciate their history and culture than when you were young.

As you're probably aware, the years seem to go by faster the older you get. Travel can help slow down those years by giving you memories that prevent one year from bleeding into another. Sometimes, it's easy to get comfortable in the routines and regimens of everyday life, and before we know it, five years slip by. Planning travel and actually going on the trips can help distinguish one year from another, making them seem to slow down at least a little bit.

However, not everyone likes to travel, or at least they don't like to plan and take major trips every year. You can still benefit from getting away from your busy life by going camping (or "glamping," if you're not into exploring the wide outdoors). Often, people who would rather not deal with the crowds and tourist traps of typical large-scale vacations love getting away to the mountains or other camping grounds. You don't even have to stay in a tent if you don't want to. Look for "glamping" opportunities that allow you to camp in luxurious surroundings by staying in a yurt or well-appointed tepee while still enjoying the seclusion and silence of the wilderness.

3

TAKE A ROAD TRIP

While you're considering where to go when traveling, put a road trip on your list of possibilities. Not only can driving to your destinations be significantly cheaper than flying, but you'll get to see sights you would otherwise miss. Going on a road trip allows you to really take your time getting to your final destination. This can be restorative, especially if you spend your driving time reflecting on your life or having deep conversations with friends or family.

One fun thing as you drive to your destination can be to plan your trip according to the various roadside attractions on the way. There is no shortage of quirky businesses that cater to tourists on U.S. roadways, and it can be a blast to visit them when you want to take a break from being in the car. Route 66 has dozens of fun historic places to stop, including the Gateway Arch in Missouri, Cadillac Ranch in Texas, The Milk Bottle Grocery in Oklahoma, and more. Other highways feature interesting sights such as Bishop Castle in Colorado, the Jolly Green Giant in Minnesota, and "Carhenge" in Nebraska.

There are other benefits to road trips in addition to them being less expensive and providing time for reflection. For example, you can truly get away from work because you can't be on your devices if you're driving. Even if you're a passenger, the WiFi can be spotty in rural areas of the country. It's an opportunity for you to really disconnect from busy life (and social media) as you put the miles behind you.

4

EXPLORE
SOLO ACTIVITIES

Speaking of travel, you may be reluctant to visit new places or revisit places that are meaningful to you if you don't have anyone with whom to travel. That's okay, though, because one thing you should consider doing as you age is exploring solo activities, like traveling, by yourself. While it's nice to experience travel with another person or a group of people, traveling on your own frees you up to do and see exactly what you want. Sometimes, couples aren't on the same page about the activities they enjoy while traveling. For instance, one person may want to relax near the hotel pool or on the beach while the other person may want to explore the sights or shop. When you go solo, you are in control of all aspects of your trip.

If you aren't quite ready to splurge on a solo vacation, you can explore other activities on your own, like dining out or going to a movie. These are things that people normally do with others, but there's no reason you can't engage in them on your own. In fact, doing things by yourself can actually be more fun than doing them with someone else, at least in a different way. Even with our closest friends and family members, we are often inhibited when we go out, but when we're by ourselves, that inhibition tends to go away. We enjoy things differently when no one's with us to observe and possibly judge our behaviors.

However, it's human nature to avoid going out by ourselves because we are worried about what others may think of us. Studies have shown that people stay in when they don't have someone with whom to go out rather than risk strangers thinking they're "losers" for being out alone. Of course, the perceived judgement is rarely the case, as research has also found that strangers typically have very little interest in the people around them. So, don't let your own worries about engaging in solo activities stop you from doing things you enjoy. You might actually discover you like your own company.

5

LIVE IN A
FOREIGN COUNTRY

Perhaps traveling isn't enough of an opportunity to experience the benefits of a different culture, especially if you stay in your own country. If this describes you, it might be time to consider moving abroad for a period — or for the rest of your life. Once you retire, you could finally be unencumbered enough to live anywhere you want, whether it's for a short time or permanently.

There are several ways to experience living in a foreign country without leaving your life in the U.S. completely behind. With Airbnbs all over the world, you can find a temporary home to accommodate various lengths of stay. You might even consider renting out your U.S. house as an Airbnb while you're living abroad so you can always return if things don't work out or you decide not to make your move permanent. This option can also give you an income to help pay for expenses while you're away.

Many benefits come from living in a place entirely different from where you were raised, which can be especially useful as you get older. You'll experience a new culture that can open your eyes to how others live and increase your awareness of human differences. It can be easy to stay locked in one worldview as you get older and less inclined to get out of comfort zones. Living in a foreign country helps keep you open-minded. You might discover that you crave diversity after you've spent time alongside other cultures and that living in your current city may not fulfill you as it once did. If this happens, consider making your move abroad permanent.

6

TALK TO STRANGERS

You don't have to live in a foreign country to expose yourself to different cultures and viewpoints. You probably live near many people with diverse backgrounds but don't even realize it. Fortunately, now that you're 60 years old, the axiom of not talking to strangers usually doesn't apply. Starting conversations with people you don't know can be an excellent way to bridge the gap between cultures, generations, and opinions. Unfortunately, many people don't talk to those they don't know very often, which can breed division and the feeling of disconnection.

Opportunities to talk to strangers arise almost daily, whether it's a person waiting in the same line as you or your Uber or Lyft driver. Of course, you may find someone who is unwilling to engage in conversation, but don't let this deter you. Most people will happily talk to you if you open that possibility for them. Humans generally like to talk about themselves, so asking questions about others' lives can be an excellent way to learn more about the people in your community. Expanding your horizons by meeting new people can lead to friendship, potential business connections, and shared experiences, all of which can be beneficial in your new phase of life.

Moreover, research indicates that connecting with strangers increases happiness and well-being. People are naturally social creatures, which is why the pandemic and resulting quarantines have been so hard on many of us. The fear that we'll get rejected if we initiate a conversation with someone we don't know prevents us from trying, but engaging with strangers we meet increases our feelings of belonging and connectedness. Even just brief eye contact with someone lets us know our existence is acknowledged, and we feel better about that existence as a result.

Be aware that using your mobile phone in public is a not-so-subtle indication that you don't want to engage in conversation with another person. So, put your phone away the next time you're out and about, and strike up a conversation with your barista, the other person waiting for their car's oil to be changed, or the person on the treadmill next to you in the gym. You just might be surprised at how positive you feel after the interaction.

7

TALK TO YOUR NEIGHBORS

Even your neighbors present an opportunity to socialize. While talking to strangers is a great way to learn new things, talking to your neighbors can be just as enlightening, particularly if you've never taken the time to get to know them before. In the past, neighbors spent a lot of time with each other, and everyone knew everyone else. These days, given how busy our lives are and how often people move, neighbors can sometimes go years without ever meeting each other. This may be part of the reason why the country feels so disconnected right now.

The good news is that it doesn't have to be that way, and you can be the person who takes that first step toward getting to know your neighbors better. There are many ways to bring your neighbors together, whether one at a time or as a group, but someone must be the one to initiate those activities. For example, you could bake some yummy treats and take them to each of your neighbors to invite conversation. Everyone likes to receive an unexpected gift, so a treat is a wonderful way to break the ice.

Another excellent idea is to throw a block party. If you plan it during the summer, you can have it outside so you don't have to host anyone in your house, and the activity in the street will hopefully get curious neighbors out socializing. You supply the main dish (think barbecue or catered sandwiches) and have everyone else bring a side dish or drink. Plan some games for kids to play while the adults talk and get to know each other. The nice part about this type of party is that no one has far to go when it's time to head home.

When thinking about the types of things that can bring a neighborhood closer together, crime prevention is at the top of the list. You all want to live in a safe area and can invest in keeping it that way. Organizing a neighborhood watch group can accomplish your goal of talking to your neighbors and everyone's goal of looking out for each other's safety. Talk to your local police department about organizing a group.

8

START A CLUB

If crime fighting isn't for you, there are plenty of other types of clubs you can start, allowing you to create a group from scratch with common interests. When you join an existing club (also a good idea), you may feel like an outsider at first, especially if there are members who have been around since the beginning. Starting a new club, though, gives you the opportunity to be in on the ground level, just like all other members. You can organize it however you want so that it's tailored to your goals.

To start a club, think about your hobbies and what you like to do with others. These could be playing games or cards, reading and discussing books, gardening, birdwatching, traveling, sports like golf or bowling, and more. The possibilities are truly endless! Once you choose your focus, invite people to join. You might already know some people who share your passion and will join right away. However, if your club has a narrow focus, you may have to expand your invitations to people you don't know.

There are plenty of places to advertise your club, both in the real world and online. Your community center and local grocery stores likely have bulletin boards where you can post a flyer, or you can post a digital advertisement on a website like meetup.com or Craigslist. No matter where you post, it's a good idea to have people call to get more information before telling them where you meet until you get a good idea of who is inquiring about the club.

9

REVIVE AN OLD HOBBY

Starting a club focused on your passion is just one idea, though. When you don't have a job to go to every day, you'll find that you have some time to fill; and what better way to fill it than by reviving a hobby you used to enjoy before the rest of life got in the way? This is the perfect time to think about hobbies you loved in the past but haven't had time to pursue. Perhaps you used to create homemade cards for the people in your life, but once you had a full-time job and a family, you couldn't devote the time necessary to keep making them. Or, maybe you love baking, but every night after work you've been too exhausted to consider working in the kitchen.

Once you retire, even if it's a few years away yet, you can organize your schedule to be able to engage in your previous hobbies and feel free to spend as much time as you want doing them. After all, you've worked hard to get to the point where you can spend your time doing the things you love, so don't feel guilty about doing them!

If you're a little lost as to what hobbies you used to love, particularly if it's been a long time since you've been able to do them, think about what you used to love doing as a child. Our hobbies often stem back to the things we found pleasure in when we last had significant amounts of time on our hands. Did you like to paint or draw? Were you always going on hikes or bike rides? Did your parents have to tear you away from video games or movies? These are all hints as to what you might still enjoy doing today. Of course, you're not committed or restricted to any one hobby. Try as many as you want until you find the one that speaks to you.

10

FIND A NEW HOBBY

Speaking of trying out different hobbies, while you're thinking about a previous passion you would like to reignite, you may also want to consider finding a new hobby or two--something you've never tried before. Maybe you're no longer fulfilled by hobbies you used to enjoy, and that's why you don't participate in them anymore. Or, maybe you can no longer physically participate in an old hobby. In these cases, discovering a new hobby makes perfect sense.

Finding a new hobby is fun because you get to try out new activities that look interesting to you. There are so many things to try that you're bound to discover one or two that resonate with what you find enjoyable. Check out the classes offered through your local recreation or community center. This is a great place to start your search. You can also ask your friends what they do for fun and ask to tag along one day to see if you like it too. In fact, this is a wonderful way to incorporate socializing with your hobby.

The internet can also provide you with a wealth of information on any hobby you can imagine. YouTube videos, blogs, how-to articles, club pages, and other resources can give you an idea of what is involved in a hobby before you get started. That way, you can avoid spending a ton of money on an activity you discover you don't really enjoy.

Some of the more popular hobbies that might be of interest include learning to play a musical instrument, learning a new language, experimenting with cooking techniques, participating in new sports (pickleball, anyone?), growing your own food, playing games (board games or online games), scouting for antiques or collectibles, decorating cakes, sculpting pottery, and traveling. But don't let that list limit you. There are as many possibilities as interests out there, so keep looking!

11

READ BOOKS YOU'VE NEVER HAD TIME TO READ

One hobby that often seems to fall by the wayside as our lives become packed with responsibilities and commitments is reading. Of course, not everyone likes to read, but those who do often create long lists of books they want to read once they have time. Well, don't put them off any longer! Just as you shouldn't feel guilty for reviving or starting a hobby, you shouldn't feel guilty for taking time to simply read for pleasure.

This is one activity that can be done without spending a single penny, since you can access all the books you can imagine through your local library for free. As such, reading is a fantastic hobby for anyone on a tight budget who needs to find inexpensive hobbies to fill their days. Even if you're not into reading books, you can access magazines and newspapers at the library, too, which can be a healthy way to keep up on current events without wading through misinformation on social media.

You can get back into a reading habit by re-reading a book you loved when you were younger, or you can start by reading that blockbuster novel everyone is talking about. Either way, dedicate some time each day to reading until you've turned it into a habit that is an integral part of your day. You may find the time you spend reading gets longer and longer each day when you discover a book you just can't put down because it's captured your imagination!

12

START A BLOG OR VLOG

Believe it or not, you've lived a unique life from which other people can learn. Even if you don't want to teach anyone about the life lessons you've learned, you still have experiences that should be shared. Starting a blog or a vlog can provide you with an outlet to publish your thoughts. A blog is a collection of informal written entries that are often a part of a website. However, you can have a blog that is independent of a website and can be made public or kept private. The nice part about blogging is that you can choose your audience, so if you just want to write for your friends and family, you can.

A vlog is a video blog and is an excellent option for people who don't enjoy writing or who are just more comfortable sharing their ideas verbally. As with blogs, with vlogs, you can usually control your audience, but it will depend on where you publish. YouTube is a popular platform for vlogs, and there are settings that can keep your episodes private or shared with select viewers.

The best aspect of starting a blog or a vlog is that you can talk about whatever you want. Maybe you want a way to express your observations or you're looking for a place to hold your memories as you reflect back on your life. Perhaps you're involved in politics or a specific sport and you want to provide commentary on events that occur in those realms. Or, maybe you want to talk about your hobby and invite others who share your interest to engage with you. Whatever your goal is, a blog or vlog can help accomplish it.

There are plenty of free blog hosting sites on the internet, or, if you already have a website of your own, you can easily add a blog. It's a little more difficult to find a free vlog hosting site, but again, many vloggers use YouTube and the newer TikTok to upload their videos for free. Spend some time reading blogs and watching vlogs to see how best to format them, especially if you plan to publish them to the public.

13

TEACH A CLASS

In your 60 years on Earth, you've accumulated a significant amount of knowledge, and you likely have some specialized knowledge based on your career as well. Why not pass that knowledge onto other people by teaching a class? These days, there are many opportunities, both on and offline, to teach classes. In fact, you can even make money by selling a course through an online course provider. Most of these providers offer course templates to help you organize your material and create lessons for students. You usually don't teach these courses in person but instead record them so students can access them on demand. You receive a royalty fee from the provider whenever your course is purchased.

If teaching in person is more your style, consider becoming a substitute for your local school district or a private school. There is a shortage of substitutes in most areas right now, so you'd also be providing a valuable service to both the schools and the students. You will need to undergo a background check and have your fingerprints taken before you'll be able to substitute in any school, and many districts require you to have your substitute teacher's license, which can be acquired through your state's education department.

Community colleges also often have openings for guest teachers, and if you're interested in teaching classes about your hobbies or other interests, community and recreation centers typically have openings as well. Museums, nature centers, animal rescue organizations, and summer camps are other places that may have a need for teachers.

You'll never lack opportunities to teach if you do it on a volunteer basis, as churches, community centers, nursing homes, retirement homes, and other facilities are always looking for volunteer teachers. If you want to get paid for your efforts, though, schools and online course providers are your best bet.

14

THROW A PARTY

Turning 60 offers a fabulous reason to throw a party. You don't even really need a reason to host a party, but a milestone birthday is certainly a good one! Don't wait for someone to offer to throw a party for you because, if you plan it yourself, you can have the exact party you want. Everyone should throw a party for themselves at least once in their lives, so if you haven't done it yet, start planning!

If your birthday isn't something you feel like partying over, wait until you retire and hold a blowout bash then. Certainly, leaving the workforce after you've spent so many years there is worth celebrating. Plus, it might be one of the last times you'll get to see some of your coworkers, as they'll likely continue to work while you move onto the new phase of your life. Retirement is a milestone you'll probably only achieve once, so you might as well mark the occasion with a party to remember!

Another party you might consider organizing once you turn 60 is a family reunion. If you're like most people, you have family members scattered all over the country, and you don't get to see each other very often. By planning a family reunion for a year or so away, you can give your family members enough time to clear their calendars and get time off from work to attend. You'll also have plenty of time to take care of the little things that turn fun parties into incredible parties, including food, games, music, centerpieces, decorations, and more. You might even consider organizing outings for your out-of-state relatives as well.

As mentioned, you don't even need a reason to throw a party. If you just feel like getting your friends together one weekend, do it! Everyone is busy, but everyone also loves a party. If you plan it, they will come!

15

GO TO A
SCHOOL REUNION

Speaking of a good party, you probably have a school reunion coming up, whether you're on the planning committee or not. Even if you haven't gone to a reunion before, or if it's been years since you last attended one, consider going to your next class get-together. Many people avoid class reunions because they're afraid of what their former classmates will think of them now that they're older. However, by the time you get to your 40th or 50th class reunion, people are usually just glad to see each other and catch up on their lives.

No matter what you ended up doing for a living or how different you look now than you did then, a class reunion is a unique opportunity to spend time with people who knew you when you were a child and teenager. There aren't many people in the world who can reminisce about your formative years, and bringing back those memories can be powerful, especially in your older years. You have probably forgotten many of the things you did in high school, but since everyone has different memories, your classmates can recall events that you've forgotten, and you can do the same for them.

Even if you're friends with some of your classmates on social media, nothing beats getting together with them in person. In fact, knowing about their lives on social media should give you even more confidence to meet up with them in real life because, unlike reunions in the past, you already have a familiarity. There may be some old friends who aren't on social media who show up to the reunion, and they're a bonus. Seeing the people in person you've remained friends with throughout the years, even if only on social media, is the true gift of class reunions.

16

REDECORATE

Depending on how long you've lived in your home, it could be time for a new look. Redecorating your home, or even just a room in your house, can make it feel brand new, which can make you feel refreshed and content. Styles change so quickly that it's likely your decor is out of date, even if you've tried to keep up with trends. Think about how you feel when you decorate for a holiday. You're probably excited, but it also makes your space look different, at least for a while. Change is good for your self-esteem and positive outlook.

Redecorating a room or your whole house has the same effect, but for a longer amount of time. When a holiday ends, you usually take down your decorations and your house returns to normal, which can feel depressing. However, when you redecorate, you don't have to change again until things begin to feel stale, if ever. You may discover that your new design is perfect and makes you feel content in your space. As long as it continues to do that, there's no reason to change.

You don't need to overhaul every part of your house at once. You might not have the funds to do that anyway. However, making small changes a bit at a time will create progress toward your final design. Start with replacing a couch or the drapes in your front room, continue with the tables, paint the walls, and finish with artwork and accessories. Eventually, you'll have a redecorated room that matches your new phase of life.

If you're still working, consider redecorating your office to allow you to finish out your time with the company in style. It can be difficult to push through the last few years of work, especially if you've set a retirement date. Redecorating can give you the incentive you need to finish strong and remain as happy as possible in your position. Even if you're working from home, an overhaul of your home office can do wonders for your morale.

17

BUY (OR RENT) THE CAR YOU'VE ALWAYS WANTED

Most of us have drooled over a vehicle at some point in our lives. Even if we're not car enthusiasts, we know what we like, and sometimes the vehicles we covet aren't always practical. As a result, our dream car stays a dream, and we buy cars that are more conducive to our lifestyle. This is why we choose a minivan over that Corvette.

Now that you're 60, though, if it won't wreck you financially, it's time to splurge and buy that car you've always wanted. You probably don't need a family vehicle anymore, and if you're retired, you don't need a commuter. Of course, you may want to keep an everyday car available for errands and road trips, but buying that sportscar or four-wheel-drive rock crawler can give you a sense of fulfillment like no other. Certainly, life is about more than material belongings, but finally getting your dream car can be representative of a lifetime of hard work.

If you don't have the money to buy your dream car, that's okay! You can still experience the joy of driving it by either taking one for a free test drive or renting one for a day or weekend. Some dealerships, especially those with exotic cars, may require income information to make sure you're serious about buying, but others don't have that stipulation. Call around until you find one that will allow you to test drive the car you've always wanted, at least for a few minutes.

Renting the car of your dreams is also a possibility, and in many cities, there are companies that rent out exotic and rare cars for a day or two at a time. While these experiences are often expensive, they're much cheaper than buying one. This is an excellent way to have that car in your driveway for a few hours — in between your drives, of course!

18

ADOPT A PET

Nothing adds joy to life like a pet. This is scientifically true, especially for older adults. You not only gain loyal companionship when you adopt a pet, but you also get the mental health benefits that come with caring for another being. There are dozens of studies that prove the health benefits attached to having a dog or cat as a pet, but there is evidence that these benefits extend to other types of pets as well. So, don't limit yourself to a dog or cat if neither of those species appeals to you.

Medical benefits of having a pet include lower blood pressure, cholesterol levels, and heart rate, all of which are instrumental in keeping you out of the doctor's office as you age. Just petting a dog or cat has been shown to calm a person's nerves and anxiety, no matter how old you are. Additionally, both dogs and cats are known to be sensitive to people's moods, and they can cheer you up when you're feeling depressed. There's nothing more restorative than cuddling with an animal when you're upset or anxious.

Caring for an animal also gives owners a routine that can help stave off boredom and isolation. You may establish a regimen that includes walking your dog every morning or taking them to a dog park once a week. This gives you opportunities to meet and converse with other people who have dogs. Cats are more independent, but you'll still need to feed them on time, as anyone who has a cat already knows. They certainly won't let you sleep in if their bowl is empty!

Consider adopting a pet from a rescue facility, since they are filled with animals that need homes. However, if you're looking for a specific type of animal to fit your lifestyle, you may need to look outside of rescue operations. Check want-ads for breeders or look for breed-specific rescues to find an animal that's right for you. If you're not ready to adopt yet, think about volunteering at a rescue facility, where you'll get all the benefits of being around animals without having to take them home with you.

19

BE PRACTICAL

Whether we want to or not, there are some things you must do as you turn 60 years old. These are the practical things that ensure our golden years are both as fulfilling and secure as possible. Taking a moment to get these things done will free up your time for fun things later.

20

CREATE A WILL

No one wants to think about dying. However, as you go through the process of creating a will, that's all you're considering for the time being. Given life's uncertainties, it's important for you to ensure your wishes are followed after you pass away. If you die without a will, the state decides how your property and assets are distributed, which is likely very different from how you would distribute them.

A will not only guarantees that your property and assets go to the people you want them to , but it also names an executor to take care of your estate (closing accounts, paying off debts, etc.), provides care for any dependents, and reduces family conflicts that can arise from property and asset division. Emotions run high in the aftermath of a death in the family and can result in hurt feelings and recriminations if a will isn't present to specify exactly how you want your property and assets divided.

Just writing down your wishes is not enough to make sure your will is legal. While some states allow handwritten wills to stand following a person's death, it can make the process more difficult and lead to legal challenges. The best way to create a legally binding will that addresses everything you need handled following your death is to have one created by a lawyer who knows how to ensure your wishes are followed to the letter.

In addition to a will, you'll also want to consider creating a living will, which keeps your property and assets in your control unless you become incapacitated and are unable to make decisions about your care and financial assets. There are some assets like retirement accounts, jointly owned property, and life insurance policies that aren't covered by a will that are included in a living will, so if you have these assets, you'll want to set up a living will to ensure they are distributed according to your wishes.

Finally, make sure your beneficiaries for all policies are up to date and that you've designated a durable power of attorney for healthcare to allow someone to make medical decisions on your behalf if you're unable to do so. Consider an advance health care directive that provides instructions on how to handle your care if certain medical conditions are present, as well as physician's orders for life sustaining treatment (POLST) to explain the treatment you want to receive in the event of an emergency.

21

PREPARE FOR MEDICARE

If you're just now turning 60 years old, you still have five years until you're eligible for Medicare; believe it or not, though, you need to start preparing for the transition to government-sponsored healthcare. You automatically become eligible for premium-free Medicare Part A when you turn 65, as long as you or your spouse have paid Medicare taxes for at least 10 years. If you or your spouse haven't paid Medicare taxes for at least 10 years, you can still buy Part A. Medicare Part A covers inpatient hospital care, skilled nursing, nursing home care, hospice care, and home health care (with restrictions).

However, just because you automatically qualify for Medicare doesn't mean you're automatically enrolled in the plan. Your enrollment period opens three months before you turn 65 and lasts for seven months, ending four months after your birthday. You'll also likely want to purchase Medicare Part B, which covers preventive services, ambulance services, durable medical equipment, and mental health services, and Medicare Part D, which covers prescription medications.

You can also choose Medicare C, which is sold by private insurance companies and eliminates the need for both Medicare B and D. These plans are often more comprehensive than Medicare B and D, but you'll also usually pay a higher premium. This is one reason you'll want to start planning for Medicare early, as you'll need to make these decisions before your 65th birthday to avoid late enrollment fees and penalties.

22

MAKE A RETIREMENT PLAN

Retirement for you may still be a few years away, but now's the time to start planning for it. Even if you have no intentions to stop working anytime soon, it's important to have at least a basic plan in case your circumstances change. The first step is to determine the age at which you want to retire. To receive full Social Security benefits, you must wait until you're 67 years old to retire (for those born in 1960 or after); however, if you don't need the payments when you're eligible to receive full benefits, you can continue to increase your Social Security payment until age 70, so waiting another three years to retire can be to your benefit.

It's also critical for you to examine your investments and when they begin paying out benefits. For example, if you have a traditional IRA or 401(k) plan, you must begin taking minimum distributions at age 72. If you don't take a minimum payment, you'll have to pay a 50% penalty on the amount you should have taken. As such, make sure you revisit your investments with a financial planner to ensure you don't miss any required minimum distribution amounts that could affect your retirement income.

In fact, consulting a financial planner when you turn 60 is highly recommended for various reasons. They will help you determine how much income you'll need in retirement to maintain your current lifestyle, and they'll assess your resources to calculate your retirement date. You may find that you can retire earlier than you thought or that you'll need to work a few years more. Either way, starting the process early can ensure you have enough time to adjust your investments, income, and expectations before actually retiring.

Furthermore, part of your preparation for retirement may include paying off large expenses and creating a budget that will allow you to live comfortably after you stop working. These things may take some time to complete, so beginning the process when you're turning 60 is a great way to make sure you're fully prepared when your retirement date arrives.

23

PAY OFF YOUR DEBTS

As you think about retirement, you should also work toward paying off debts, especially automobile loans, credit cards, personal loans, and other types of debts that have high interest rates. These debts will eat into your savings and income, particularly after you retire and have a fixed income. You may want to talk to a financial advisor to help you determine how much you should put toward your debt to retire it before you retire because you may end up needing to work for a couple more years to be debt free going into retirement.

As far as your mortgage goes, you might not have enough time before retirement to pay it off. While you might consider taking some money out of your 401(k) or IRA to pay it off, this is almost never a good idea, especially if you're not 59½ years old yet, as you'll incur a hefty penalty for pulling it out early. If you're already 60 or older, the money should stay in your account if it's earning a higher rate of interest than what you're paying on your mortgage. As always, check with a financial expert to help guide you as you pay off your debt.

Additionally, avoid taking on new debt if possible. This is especially important if you're going to have a minimal amount of discretionary funds when you retire. Until you really know what your finances will look like after you stop working, you shouldn't buy a new car, charge a significant amount on a credit card (unless you pay it off right away), or take on a larger mortgage than you already have. You may consider taking out a home equity line of credit if you need home improvements or repairs, since it will be at a much lower rate than credit cards or personal loans.

24

GET (OR STAY) FIT

Even if you've always been healthy, when you turn 60, you'll want to start paying closer attention to your fitness and health. The reason for this is simple: as we age, our bodies begin to break down, so it's vital for us to do what we can to keep our bones, muscles, and organs as strong as possible. According to the CDC, falls are the number one cause of injuries in older Americans. By keeping ourselves strong and healthy, we can reduce our likelihood of becoming injured or falling in the first place.

Although there's no need to become an elite athlete, regular exercise is critical, especially as you age. Lifting light weights, walking, swimming, yoga, and other low-impact exercises will ensure you keep your muscles active and your joints flexible. Not only will exercise help keep you from getting injured in a fall, but it will also make everyday activities like chores and playing with grandkids easier.

Your diet plays an important role in your health as well, as it has for your entire life. However, as you get older, your body will require different nutrients than it once did. For example, adding more fiber to your diet can lower cholesterol, reduce constipation, and lower the risk of heart disease, diabetes, and colon cancer. Consider taking a multivitamin formulated for seniors to get the right amount of nutrients you need, but talk to your doctor first for suggestions and advice.

In fact, one of the best things you can do when you reach 60 years old is to get a full physical with blood work from your primary care physician, especially if you haven't had one in a while. This will give you and your medical team baseline readings on your health so if anything changes, they'll be able to immediately intervene to correct issues.

Of course, as always, drink plenty of water, seek medical care when appropriate, and take plenty of naps. These tips will ensure you are always ready for anything that comes your way, whether it's your family wanting to take you to dinner or your best friend inviting you on a road trip across the country.

25

DOWNSIZE

Now that you may have (mostly) raised children, if they've moved out of your house, you probably have a lot of extra space and belongings you don't really need anymore. It may be time to consider downsizing in terms of your belongings and your actual dwelling. Many people find that as they get older, they don't need as much "stuff." Living in a cluttered home can be stressful and even dangerous (if there are tripping hazards, for example).

There are plenty of ways to reduce your belongings, from selling them at a garage sale or online to donating them to people in need. Garage sales, flea markets, and consignment shops are excellent local options for you to offer unneeded belongings for sale, but you can also try Craigslist, Nextdoor, or other online platforms that connect people who have things with people who need things.

For the extra-ambitious sellers out there, look at eBay or other national and international selling websites. You'll find a much wider audience for your items and may be able to fetch a better price, but you'll also probably have to ship them, which requires added costs and effort. If you're looking for a nice part-time job, though, online sales could be a great way to earn a little extra cash and downsize at the same time.

Once you've purged your belongings through sales and donations, you'll probably find that you have too much space on your hands. This could be the time to think about selling your house and moving into a smaller one. Many older people discover that stairs and yards are no longer as attractive as they once were and prefer to live in a single-level home with a small yard, or without a yard at all. Ground-level condos and apartments are excellent options, especially if the outside maintenance is taken care of by an HOA or management company.

26

GET ORGANIZED

While you're in the downsizing mood, take the time to organize yourself as well, particularly if you don't plan on moving anytime soon. As you reduce the clutter in your home, find a home for everything that's left, so when you need it, you'll have no trouble locating it. This becomes more important as you age and become less mobile. Make sure the things you need frequently are easy to reach and that nothing stays out that could become a tripping hazard.

Give yourself time to thoroughly go through everything because you'll probably need to make some hard decisions as you organize your home. Ask yourself what things you really must keep as opposed to what you may be keeping out of guilt or nostalgia. Now is the time to make your life as comfortable as possible, and one way to do this is to reduce the weight of disorganization and clutter from your shoulders.

Remember that you don't have to tackle everything at once, either. Start small with just a drawer or a closet and keep going from there. Soon, you'll have all your rooms organized so you can focus your energy on other tasks, most of which are probably more fun than organizing. Taking the time to declutter and organize now means you won't have to do it when you get older. Plus, you'll be doing your heirs a favor as well, so they'll have less to do when you pass away.

Rooms and spaces that usually become disorganized over time and may require some attention include kitchen cabinets, closets, offices, spare bedrooms, garages, and storage areas. Start with the spaces that bother you the most, and once you realize how good it feels to be organized, you'll find it easier to tackle the other spaces.

27

EMBRACE NEW TECHNOLOGY

Did you know there are many new gadgets out there that can make your life easier? Even if you prefer to do things the "old school" way, you might be surprised at how simple technology can be to adopt and integrate into your life. For instance, installing a smart speaker in your home can give you information at your fingertips you'd otherwise have to look up online or in books. Certainly, reading and surfing online might be enjoyable hobbies of yours, but how about turning off lights you left on without even getting out of bed? You can do that with a smart speaker and a few smart lightbulbs, all of which are simple to set up.

Convenience is just one of the reasons you may want to embrace new technology. There are safety considerations as well. For instance, if you don't already have a mobile phone, you probably should get one, especially if you live by yourself. As mentioned earlier, falls become increasingly common as we get older, and if you don't have a mobile phone you carry with you, it could be difficult for you to get help when you need it. The same is true when you drive or travel on your own. The technology is available to make you safer, so why not use it?

28

JOIN AARP

If you haven't already, become a member of the American Association of Retired Persons (AARP). You're eligible at any age, but the group caters to people over 50 (although many don't consider that to be old enough to belong to an organization designed to benefit "seniors"). However, there are numerous benefits to joining, many of which can save you money. A membership is just $16 per year, and for all the discounts, services, and information you get, this is one of few true bargains left. You can even get a lower price ($12!) if you sign up for auto-renewal or a long-term membership plan.

Even better is the fact that you can add your spouse to your plan for free, which means you're actually getting two memberships for the price of one. The amount of money you save on discounts and coupons will more than cover the $16 per year and can really add up if you are diligent about using your benefits whenever possible.

There are 15 benefit categories for AARP that offer opportunities to save money, volunteer, and learn. These include travel, insurance, entertainment, restaurants, shopping, groceries, caregiving, magazines, and more. The most popular benefits among members include travel, dental, hearing, grocery coupons, rent-a-car, vision, and games. However, there is likely something available for everyone, even if those popular categories don't hold your interest.

Another great benefit of AARP is that it offers reliable information about complicated issues like Medicare, Social Security, and financial planning. AARP is well-known for its thorough research on issues that affect senior citizens and for making complex subjects easier to understand. Most of this information is available without a membership, so if you don't join, you can still take advantage of the group's research and information for free. However, you won't get the *AARP Magazine*, a monthly publication included in your membership that provides articles, features, advertising, and offers of interest to people over 50.

29

IMPROVE YOURSELF

Self-improvement is something most of us have worked on for years, but when you turn 60, it's time to really focus on you. It's likely you've spent many decades taking care of other people, and now you can start being good to yourself. It's not necessary for you to make all these changes at once, which would be overwhelming, to say the least. Instead, choose one or two to work on at a time and you'll be glad you did.

30

CULTIVATE RELATIONSHIPS

As we age, it can be easy to neglect relationships because we get so busy doing other things. However, it's critical for you to not only pay attention to your relationships but take steps to strengthen them as well.

You might also be experiencing grandparenthood at this age, which means you'll want to spend a lot of time with your grandchildren. This will probably come naturally when they're little, but as your grandkids get older, keep doing the things they have always enjoyed doing with you. You're making memories with them they'll cherish for a lifetime. This is also true for your own kids. Now that they're grown, you might find yourself not spending as much time with them as you once did, but they still need you. Dedicate some time to your adult kids without your grandchildren so you both can enjoy this season in life.

If your parents are still alive, you might already be heavily involved in their caretaking. Continue strengthening those bonds and spending as much time as possible with them outside of medical appointments and caretaking duties. This can be challenging, especially with the other relationships you must nurture, but as you're aware, their time is short. You'll treasure for the rest of your life the time you take now to truly be present with them.

Married couples can do several things to make their connection stronger after the age of 60. For example, marriage counseling isn't just for when you're having trouble in your marriage. It can be a way to rediscover your relationship with each other now that your children have grown and it's just the two of you again. Keep up with date nights, join clubs together, travel, or simply just spend time talking. You may be surprised at what you learn!

31

MAINTAIN YOUR SOCIAL LIFE

Once you quit working, you might find that your social circle shrinks, particularly if you don't intentionally work to maintain it. Keep planning activities with your friends, even if they're still working, and try to establish new routines that keep friends in your life. For example, you may want to have a standing coffee date with one friend every Friday morning and lunch with another every Wednesday.

After you retire, you might find that many of your friends who are still working aren't as available to visit with you as you are with them. Don't let this stop you from being social. Join clubs and make new friends who have similar interests and schedules. Attend concerts by your favorite bands to meet other people who enjoy the same music. Take classes that bring you in contact with others in the same stage of life. It might seem daunting to make new friends when you're 60 years old, but there are plenty of ways to meet new people, particularly when you have access to the internet.

Traveling with friends can also be a great way to maintain your social life after retirement. You may already be planning to travel with your spouse or family members, but don't forget about seeing the sights with friends. It can be a fantastic way to develop close relationships with them as well as create memories that can be shared for a lifetime.

Be sure to budget some money for your social life so you can continue to do the things you enjoy. If you're worried about your money running out after you retire, it can be tempting to cut out social activities to save cash. However, this is not healthy for you because you need friends and fun in your life. You don't have to spend a lot of money to keep your social life active. There are many free and low-cost activities at community centers that allow you to remain active as you age.

32

DROP TOXIC
RELATIONSHIPS

While cultivating relationships is vital to fight loneliness and isolation as you get older, there are some relationships that should actually be dropped because they're toxic and only add stress to your life. If you've been hanging onto toxic relationships out of a sense of obligation or guilt, now's the time to let them go. Remember that you're working on yourself now, and that means you shouldn't stay in touch with people who aren't supporting you in that endeavor.

Social media has some fantastic benefits, including the ability to keep up with people who live far away or who you might not have time to see in person very often. However, there are many downsides to social media as well. For instance, you might find that you compare yourself to everyone else on the internet, which isn't healthy, especially when you consider that most people only show the good parts of their life online. If someone's social media activity makes you feel bad about yourself, unfriend them, or, at the very least, remove them from your newsfeed. Almost all social media platforms have controls that allow you to stay friends with people but not see their posts. Take advantage of these controls to detoxify your social media.

Dropping your toxic relationships can extend to family as well. If you're keeping someone in your life just because they're related to you, it's time to reconsider. Don't feel bad about quietly bowing out of those relationships, particularly if they are causing you stress or anxiety. Blood relation doesn't give anyone the right to prevent you from living your best life. Again, you may not have to remove them entirely from your life, but silencing them on social media and limiting contact can help you take control of your inner peace.

Now that your kids are grown, you might find that you and your spouse are no longer compatible or that you are better off as friends. Counseling may help you rediscover your passion for each other, but if not, a divorce might be necessary for your well-being. No one goes into a marriage expecting to get a divorce, but if the relationship is no longer healthy, it could be something you consider, allowing both of you to start fresh.

33

GO TO THERAPY

Therapy isn't just for people who are struggling in life. It can serve as an outlet for anyone who just needs someone to help talk things through. Even if you're married or have a best friend to whom you tell everything, a therapist can still be beneficial because they're an impartial third party who can help you learn new things about yourself without passing judgment. Therapists are trained to ask the right questions that can lead to self-discovery, which can then lead to a more fulfilling life.

If you are struggling with relationships, retirement, or just getting older, a therapist can definitely be beneficial because they can give you a way to explore feelings in a safe and healthy manner. As you age, you're going to experience many new and unfamiliar things, which can cause turmoil in your life. A therapist will help you work through and give perspective on these issues. You can certainly try to muddle through these changes on your own, but why? There are experts who are skilled at helping you deal with things that are causing problems in your life or relationships.

Therapy may be particularly helpful for you if you live alone and don't have someone to talk to every day. Just having someone listen to you and provide advice or compassion can be a way to relieve yourself of burdens you're carrying. Therapy is not just for young people or for couples. It's for anyone who wants to share their thoughts, ideas, and problems with someone trained to help work through them in a positive way.

You'll be able to choose between individual and group therapy, each of which offer various benefits. For instance, individual therapy is private, while group therapy offers the opportunity for you to learn from others who are in the same stage of life and who may be having many of the same experiences. To get started, though, it's best to begin with a one-on-one session with a counselor who can then help you determine which format is best for your needs.

34

GIVE FORGIVENESS

One of the best things you can do to improve your own health as you get older is to forgive others for pain they've caused you in the past. This can be challenging, since we tend to hang onto hurt feelings whether we intend to or not. However, research indicates that forgiveness can reduce the risk of a heart attack, improve cholesterol levels, and lower blood pressure. There is also evidence that learning to let go of negative feelings helps reduce pain, anxiety, depression, and stress levels. What's more is that the link between forgiveness and health becomes critical as you get older.

Holding onto pain and anger only hurts you, especially if the other person doesn't even acknowledge the issue. If they're oblivious to pain they've caused, you're the only one suffering. Letting go of hurt feelings, whether the other person deserves forgiveness or not, returns control of the situation to you instead of letting them hold you hostage to that pain.

You don't even have to tell the other person you forgive them unless you want to. However, you should acknowledge your actions by writing down that you forgive that person in a journal or diary to empower your conscious choice to provide forgiveness. It is a choice to forgive someone or not, and making the choice to do it restores your control and power along with your health.

You may find that telling the other person you forgive them lifts the burden you've been holding onto even more. If you can't talk to them in person or over the phone, write them a letter. In the letter, empathize with what they may have been going through at the time they hurt you and explain that you understand no one is perfect. Don't rehash the event or situation since that may end up negating the forgiveness. Even if you don't want a continuing relationship with that person, remember that you're forgiving them for your own benefit, not theirs.

35

VOLUNTEER

A great way to improve your overall sense of well-being is to volunteer your time giving back to your community. A study conducted by the Corporation for National Community Service found that older Americans who spend time volunteering live longer and have fewer disabilities than those who don't volunteer. In fact, the research discovered that volunteering led to higher levels of happiness and satisfaction than money or education, especially for older adults. This can be attributed to the health benefits you get from the social, mental, and physical aspects of volunteering.

After you retire, you'll have dozens of volunteer opportunities available to you, whether it's through a church or a community-based program. Schools, shelters, food pantries, nursing homes, and other facilities all need volunteers and welcome older adults doing it for altruistic reasons. You may need to undergo a background check for some volunteer roles, particularly in schools, but that's often the only necessary requirement for most opportunities.

Volunteering not only helps you live healthier and happier days but also provides a valuable service to your community. Many organizations, such as museums and hospitals, couldn't operate without volunteers because there are so many jobs that need done; they need people just like you. Try different volunteer roles until you find the ones that fit best with your skills and passion. You're sure to discover ways you can give back to your community you didn't know were possible.

This also offers you the chance to bridge the generation gap by volunteering with organizations that serve young people, including schools, camps, and clubs. You'll give young people the opportunity to have good experiences with older adults, and you'll learn more about what is important to younger generations. This perspective can improve your interactions with the young people in your life and, in turn, make your time with them more enjoyable.

36

GET INVOLVED WITH A CAUSE YOU CARE ABOUT

If you don't want to volunteer, you can still get involved with a cause you care about through donations or activism. For example, politics may be important to you, especially given the current climate in the country. Perhaps you want to support a specific candidate in a local race or work to get a bill passed in the legislature. Political parties and organizations looking to get bills on the ballot are always looking for people who are passionate about their position or cause to help them get the word out to voters.

Activism is another activity that has gained popularity in recent years, with the rise of several movements that affect minorities, marginalized populations, and animals. If you feel strongly about a cause, there are many ways you can get involved, from attending rallies and marches to getting petitions signed and knocking on doors to inform voters about the cause.

You may be tempted to think that activism is a young person's game, but anyone of any age can get involved with a cause they care about in a way that works for them. If you don't feel comfortable attending a rally, that's not the only way you can participate. Search for an organization that supports your cause online, contact them, and ask what opportunities they offer to get involved. If that organization doesn't have something that fits your needs, another one will.

If you do decide to attend rallies and marches, be sure to take steps to keep yourself safe while you're there. Try to go with another person so you have someone with you in case something happens while you're there. Let someone know you're attending and have a plan for getting there and getting home. If a rally turns violent, leave as soon as you can, and make sure you get out of the situation safely.

37

BECOME A MENTOR

Another way you can get involved in your community is to become a mentor to another person. While there are many programs that will allow you to mentor a child or a teen, you can also mentor older people or even former prisoners. There are people from all walks of life who need a positive influence to help them take the right path. Young people, especially, can feel disconnected from the older people in their lives, so being someone they can talk to who's not their parent or teacher can really help them gain confidence and close the generation gap.

Not every child has a support system on which they can rely, which makes it even more important for older people to mentor young kids and teens. They need a role model who can show them how to be an adult and help with transition from childhood to adulthood. You can help them learn to perform practical tasks they might not learn in school, like banking, shopping, and budgeting, or you can just be there to support them in whatever activity they choose to do. Big Brothers Big

Sisters is an excellent place to start if you want to mentor a child or teen.

In much the same way that children learn how to be adults from observing the behavior of actual adults, former prisoners often need to learn how to be productive members of society again when they get ready to re-enter their community. You can help them re-learn the skills they need to function once they get out of prison. Many people find it challenging to transition back to freedom after having been locked up for months or even years. A mentor can assist by helping them with transportation or finding a job, clothing, food, and other resources. Most prisoners find their mentors help the most by just being there for general support when things get hard. Studies show that recidivism rates drop when former prisoners are paired with a caring mentor to help them re-enter society. Churches and community centers, along with prisons and jails, often have information on mentoring opportunities available for soon-to-be former prisoners.

38

DO SOMETHING
FOR OTHERS

You don't have to participate in a formal volunteer or mentorship program to make a positive impact in your world. You can simply do something for others whenever the mood strikes you, which in turn will help you feel good about yourself and your life. Several studies have proven that acts of kindness boost serotonin levels in your brain, which are responsible for feelings of contentment. Moreover, these acts also release endorphins, the hormone that's responsible for your body's natural high.

The good news is that your act of kindness doesn't have to be huge to produce serotonin and endorphins. It can be as simple as paying for someone else's meal or picking up trash that doesn't belong to you and throwing it away. Furthermore, you don't even have to be acknowledged for your act of kindness for it to work its magic on your brain. Just knowing you did something good for someone else is enough to make you feel good. Of course, it's always nice to be thanked for your kindness, but appreciation is not necessary to receive the positive physical benefits.

Some kind things you can do throughout your day to make another person's day better include leaving a big tip for your server at a restaurant, paying for a stranger's meal in the car behind you in a drive-through lane, complimenting someone you don't know, surprising someone you know with a gift or just your presence, let someone go in front of you in traffic or in line at a store, feeding an expired parking meter with a quarter or two, carrying someone's groceries to their car, or giving up your seat on a crowded bus to someone else. Look for small opportunities (or big ones) to lighten someone's load and you'll lighten yours as well.

39

START A GRATITUDE LIST

Just as kindness can make you healthier, gratitude can make you happier. When you express gratitude, you become more attuned to what you already have or have had that is positive in your life instead of focusing on the negatives or what you don't have. Taking time to write down what you're grateful for on a regular basis can keep you grounded in the present rather than stressing about what the future may hold. In fact, taking stock of your gifts can help you feel more positive about the future, even if you're uncertain about what lies ahead.

When you compile your gratitude list, don't just think about material things or your current relationships. Also consider events in the past that have shaped who you are. Even difficult situations may lead to gratitude, especially if those circumstances caused you to shift your focus to a new job, new city, or new relationships. For example, if you got divorced early in your life, you might be grateful for that event because it led to meeting your current spouse.

In a research study on gratitude, one group wrote weekly about things they were grateful for, another group wrote about things that bothered or negatively impacted them, and a third group wrote about both, with no instructions on whether they should be grateful or not. After 10 weeks, the people who wrote about what they were grateful for felt more optimistic about their lives than either of the other two groups. Another study involved writing a letter to properly thank someone for something they had done in the past. This action led to an immediate increase in happiness for both the giver and receiver, and the results lasted for as long as a month.

Sometimes, we can get bogged down in the sadness we encounter on a daily basis, whether in our own communities or in the world at large. Taking time to count your blessings in the form of a gratitude list can remind you that, overall, life can be good. This attitude of positivity can breed contentment where you are in life, even if you haven't achieved everything you once wanted to.

40

EXPRESS YOUR THANKS

Not only should you keep a list of things for which you're grateful, but you should also take time to express thanks to other people. On a daily basis, you come across people who do things for you, even if you never leave your house, such as people in the service industry like your mail carrier or garbage collector. There are other people who take time out of their day to help you, like a neighbor who shovels your walk or mows your lawn. There are people who hold the door for you when your hands are full and people who let you cut in line when you're in a hurry.

Sometimes, these people don't get the thanks they deserve, which is where you come in. Expressing thanks to the people who make your everyday life better in small ways will increase your satisfaction with your current stage in life. You don't have to make a grand gesture of gratitude, but going out of your way to thank someone personally will have a major impact on that person's day. For example, you can ask to speak to a manager to compliment a worker or write a letter to your mail carrier letting them know their work is appreciated.

Another way to express your thanks in an unexpected way is to write letters or emails to companies to compliment them on something great they're doing for you or your community. Perhaps a company is donating a portion of its profits to a local family that's struggling or sponsoring an event that has personal meaning to you. Letting these companies know their actions are having an impact is important for their continued community involvement.

Keep in mind that expressing your gratitude, whether in a private list or directly to someone, can make your own life happier. Telling someone "thank you" is a kind act, and as we've already discussed, being kind can lower your blood pressure and reduce depression, stress, and anxiety. Why not make someone's day by thanking them personally and improve your health at the same time?

41

REACH OUT TO A HERO

In addition to expressing gratitude, consider reaching out to someone you've admired or who has had a significant impact on your life to let them know how they influenced your decisions. We don't always realize the impact we have on other people, and knowing we changed a life or helped someone achieve more than they would have alone is extremely gratifying. In fact, it can help another person realize they have made a mark in this world.

Some of the everyday people in your life you might consider a hero include relatives, teachers, pastors, neighbors, co-workers, friends, bosses, and community leaders. Celebrities, athletes, politicians, authors, entrepreneurs, business magnates, and other famous people can also be heroes, but you might not get as much satisfaction in reaching out to them as you will if you tell someone close to you how much they have impacted your life.

Letters, phone calls, and emails are all great ways to contact someone to tell them they're your hero. No matter how you let them know, they're going to appreciate your kindness and take pride in the role they played in your personal or professional life. Don't limit your consideration to just one person, either. If there are several people who've influenced your growth and development, let them all know. Don't put this off, since you never know how long they'll be in your life.

42

LEARN TO SAY NO

While all these things can be great for your health and well-being, you don't have to do them all at once; in fact, trying to do everything at one time would be overwhelming and defeating. Sure, you might want to volunteer, be a mentor, get involved with a cause you care about, write letters to express your thanks, and reach out to a hero, but you have your limits. This is where learning how to say no comes in handy.

First, we only have so much time in a day, and even if you're retired, you're still going to need time for yourself. Saying yes to everything will leave you drained and unable to reap the benefits of your actions, no matter how inherently positive they are. Moreover, there may be some things you simply don't want to do, and that's okay. Life is too short to do things that don't make you happy or benefit you in some way. Once you reach 60 years old, if you haven't already, it's time to set boundaries, which sometimes involves saying no.

Saying yes to everything is easy, but if you say yes when you really want to say no, you're only causing problems for yourself. You may become resentful toward the person who asked you for the favor, or you will sabotage your responsibility instead of putting forth your best effort, which will end up making everyone unhappy. Plus, other people may try to take advantage of your willingness by asking you to do more, and this will only make the situation worse.

Learning to say no can be challenging, especially if you've been saying "yes" all your life. Just remember that you don't owe anyone an explanation for why you're saying no. If you want to give one, you can simply say you're setting boundaries for your own health. Most people will respect this decision and honor your efforts to take care of yourself.

43

FEED YOUR
SPIRITUAL SIDE

As people age, they tend to become more reflective and yearn to find a deeper connection to life, whether through church, nature, music, meditation, or another spiritual endeavor. In the past, older generations have valued religion to feed their spiritual side, but today's seniors often find spiritual comfort in other ways. No matter what refreshes your spirit, be sure to devote time to its practice.

While younger generations may be more focused on material things, older people have already been through that stage and often have different priorities focused on more meaningful pursuits. For some, attending church services may be a priority, while for others, an experience like fishing along the banks of an isolated river could take precedence over everything else. Still others may lose themselves in creating music or art. Whatever your spiritual practices are, make sure you plan enough time for these activities to keep yourself refreshed and content.

If you're not sure what feeds your spiritual side, explore various activities until you find it. Most churches welcome visitors who are looking for their spiritual home, and you can usually try other activities for cheap or free by renting or borrowing equipment. Think about things you've done in the past that made you feel at peace and pursue those activities again to see if that feeling can be replicated. Take the time to discover your spiritual ventures now because you'll find that this search becomes more important as you get older.

Your spiritual pursuits may be the same as your hobbies, but the key component of a spiritual endeavor is that you are able to reflect on your life and process your feelings during the activity. As such, your hobbies might not be enough to feed your spirit. Usually, spiritual activities have a metaphysical component as well, but this isn't always necessary. Find what works for you to fill your soul.

44

TAKE CLASSES

If you retire early or if you're looking for something to do in spare time, consider taking classes in subjects you find interesting to stimulate your mind and quench your thirst for knowledge. By 60, you probably know what kinds of things you want to learn about, which could be very different from the last time you were in school. Surprisingly, even the subjects you struggled with when you were younger may hold your interest now, since maturity is often necessary before people can truly grasp the importance of certain skills.

For example, you may have hated history classes in school, but now that you're older, you're finding that learning about the past is actually fascinating, particularly as it relates to your personal or familial background. This is why genealogy has become such a popular area of study for middle-aged and older people who seek to discover more about their place in history.

History is just one example of courses available to you with the advent of the internet. No longer do you have to attend classes in person if you don't want to. You can sign up for classes online and take them whenever convenient. This makes continuing education incredibly accessible to people of all ages. You don't even have to pay for many classes, with the expansion of massive open online classes or MOOCs, which are free, online, and open to anyone regardless of background or previous education.

Classes are also available through community colleges, community centers, museums, and other brick-and-mortar entities. Many colleges will even allow you to audit classes, which means you don't earn university credit for taking them, but you do gain the knowledge from them. This can make expensive college courses more affordable. However, if you have the funds available, you might as well go ahead and earn credits toward a degree. You never know when it might come in handy.

45

KEEP MENTALLY SHARP

Even if you don't go back to school or take advantage of free and low-cost courses available online, you'll want to continue to participate in activities that keep your mind sharp. Activities such as crossword puzzles, memory challenges, logic riddles, and card games can help you keep your brain active, which is important as you age since some mental decline is expected. This isn't to say that playing games will prevent dementia, but challenging your brain to keep changing itself to respond to new concepts and skills will help keep it agile.

Research has found that brain games such as those mentioned above can stave off age-related cognitive decline. One study by Advanced Cognitive Training for Independent and Vital Elderly showed that elderly participants in brain game activities continued to benefit from the reasoning, memory, and processing speed training they acquired from the games for a decade following their participation. The earlier you start playing these types of games, the better trained your brain will be as you age.

There is no need to spend a fortune on these games, either, despite what some companies may have you believe. You can get the same benefits from free games for your phone or computer as you can from expensive programs that purport to be specifically designed to help you stay mentally sharp. Once you master a game, though, it's good to move onto a new challenge to keep your brain constantly learning.

Games aren't the only activity that can keep your brain fit. Playing a musical instrument, reading stimulating material, participating in academic or philosophical discussions (as in book clubs), and writing original content (letters, stories, journal entries) can all help your brain stay healthy and active. Certain foods, like broccoli, blueberries, fish, and nuts, and getting enough sleep on a regular basis, are other influences on brain health worth your attention.

46

BREAK A HABIT

As you continually work on self-improvement, you'll probably want to break a bad habit that has been bothering you for years. Perhaps you've tried to break this habit before but weren't successful for various reasons. No matter what has led you to this habit or how long it's been with you, it's never too late to break it for good.

There's a common perception that it takes three weeks of behavior modification to break a habit or form a new one, but newer research suggests it could take longer than two months of continual behavior modification to fully let go of a habit. In fact, for some people, it can take as long as nine months to fully be free from their habit. This means if you pass the three-week mark in your effort to drop a habit but it's still with you or you know you would slip back into old patterns if you weren't vigilant, don't despair. Your brain may just need a little longer to adapt.

Habits like smoking, eating fast food, or drinking alcohol, soda, or coffee are tougher to break because they all have an addictive component to them. You not only have to break the habit, but you also must rid your body of the addictive substance and basically go through withdrawal. While this is challenging, it's not impossible, especially if you get help to do it. There are plenty of replacements for cigarettes that can help with your smoking habit, and various support groups, medications, and nutrition experts assist with fast food and beverage habits. Therapy, which is discussed in another section, can also help you break bad habits by exploring the reasons behind their existence.

You'll also discover a variety of habit-breaking aids like trackers for your phone or habit journals that can help you maintain accountability as you work to break your habit. Another way to do this is to use social media to your benefit by asking your social network for help as you go through the habit-breaking process. Your friends can hold you accountable and provide encouragement and support that may get you through the tough times.

47

FORM A NEW HABIT

Conversely, as you drop a bad habit, think about forming a new one. In fact, research has discovered it's easier to break a poor habit if you replace it with a new, positive habit. Studies have found that people who try to quit doing something are more successful if they start doing something else in its place. This is why cigarette replacements like nicotine gum and vaporizers are useful when people try to quit smoking. They can use a healthier alternative whenever they would normally smoke a cigarette.

New habits may also stick better if they're aligned with other goals you have for your life after 60. For instance, if you have the goal of getting fit, adding in a new habit of exercising every day for 20 minutes will help you accomplish your fitness goal more quickly. If your goal is to keep your mind sharp, the habit of reading every day before bed will play a role in developing mental agility.

Breaking and forming a habit are two sides of the same coin, so just as you may not break a habit in three weeks, you also shouldn't expect a new one to stick in that same time frame. Of course, some habits are more easily formed than others, especially if you're doing something you really enjoy. For example, if you love to cook at home but didn't have the time before you retired, you'll find it much easier to develop the habit of cooking instead of eating out or ordering in since you already enjoy doing it.

Other new habits you might consider forming include meeting at least one new person every week to combat isolation and loneliness, using coupons to save money instead of going to the store without a plan, snacking on healthy rather than junk food, writing in a journal daily, having screen-free time each day, getting up or going to bed earlier, or organizing your home or office. Remember to not adopt too many new habits at one time, since one change can be difficult enough.

48

TREAT YOURSELF

Yes, you read that right! After years of taking care of others and worrying about what their needs and wants, it's time for you to treat yourself. It doesn't have to be a big treat (unless you want it to be), but doing something for yourself you've always wanted to can lift your spirits and make you feel like a brand new person. Try getting a new hair style or color, which can often trigger a side of you that may have been repressed for ages. Maybe trade in your entire wardrobe for a new style that fits who you are at age 60 compared to your younger self.

Other treats can include simply eating in an expensive restaurant and indulging in a food you'd normally skip, going on a retreat, getting regular massages, or spending an entire day binging on Netflix. This is the time in your life where you get to think about you. Likely, your children are grown up, so you're not responsible for anyone except yourself. Giving yourself a treat once in a while is not just recommended; it's necessary.

Research indicates that people who regularly treat themselves can ask more of themselves regarding healthy habits and self-control. Taking time for yourself and indulging in a treat is not selfish. In fact, it's a way to prevent feelings of resentment, depletion, and anger, which all can develop when we deprive ourselves of treats. These feelings can then lead to the attitude that we deserve self-indulgence whenever and wherever we can find it. This can cause over-indulgence, which is usually unhealthy.

You don't even have to spend money to give yourself a treat. Sleep in for a little bit longer, or go test drive a vehicle you've always wanted but can't afford to buy. These things are free but can give you a sense of well-being that you can only get from splurging on something you enjoy.

49

GET COSMETIC SURGERY (IF YOU WANT)

This piece of advice is directed toward those who have been struggling with something physical preventing you from living the life you desire (which, let's be honest, is almost everyone). Most of us have something about our bodies we'd rather looked a different way. There are many modern procedures available that can correct issues we have with our bodies, and there's no reason why you shouldn't consider them as part of your self-improvement journey.

Usually, the things we don't like about our physical appearance are not very noticeable to others, but that doesn't matter. If it bothers you, it's worth looking at ways to correct it. Most procedures these days carry minimal risk for healthy people but be sure to consult with your physician before undergoing any medical procedure to ensure you're not putting yourself at unnecessary risk.

There are also many non-surgical solutions to physical conditions that have almost no risks at all. For instance, if you're concerned about a scar on your skin, there are laser treatments that can minimize the appearance of that scar, and you don't have to undergo anesthesia to get them done. You also won't have much downtime compared to a surgical procedure. If you're concerned about the way something on your body looks, talk to a doctor about both surgical and non-surgical solutions.

Sometimes, all you need to feel better about yourself is a complete makeover. A makeover might include a new haircut, new clothes, makeup, or skin treatments, or it could mean other treatments that target your specific concerns. There are many spas available that provide makeovers and allow you to indulge in sprucing up your physical appearance in preparation for your 60s. Search around online and ask for personal recommendations until you find the one that offers the package you want.

To be clear, you don't have to have cosmetic surgery, a makeover, or laser treatments, if you don't want to. However, if your self-improvement journey includes correcting the things you don't like about your body, there is no shame in taking advantage of opportunities available to you.

50

RECONSIDER YOUR CAREER

Turning 60 doesn't mean you have to slow down. In fact, this can be an excellent time to think about doing something else for the rest of your working life. You also aren't required to retire, unless you work for a company with a mandatory retirement age. Even then, you can still get another job or start a new career, especially if you're the type of person who enjoys working and doesn't want to stop. The best thing about being older is you know what you like and what you don't. So, reconsidering your career at this point may be just the thing that makes you the happiest you've ever been.

51

GET A JOB YOU LOVE

Getting a job that you love sounds simple, doesn't it? After all, if it were that easy, you would have already done it, right? Not necessarily. There are many reasons we stay in jobs we don't like, including benefits, lack of skills, a tight job market, the inability to relocate, and more. However, now that you're 60, you may find you don't have the restrictions you used to have. For example, if you kept your job just for the insurance, once you have Medicare, that won't be an issue. Your family may have prevented you from relocating, but if they're out of the house, there's no stopping you now!

If you aren't sure what job you would love, there are some ways you can find out what you're most suited to doing. First, think about your hobbies and passions. You already love doing these things, so making money from them would just be a bonus. Perhaps you love making cards for your loved ones. There are plenty of ways to sell your designs online, including Etsy and eBay. You don't even have to have elite business skills to open a company on these platforms, and there are numerous how-to guides on the internet available for free.

You can also consult a career coach to help you make the transition from one career to another. They will probably administer aptitude tests to help narrow your options, and they can assist you with revamping your resume and applying for jobs. If you haven't done this in a long time, it may be a new adventure, especially as many applications are now online. Plus, there are so many applicants per job these days, you'll want your resume to stand out. A career coach can ensure your resume gets read and lands you an interview. Speaking of the interview, if you haven't interviewed in a while, you'll want to practice that with your coach as well.

52

START A BUSINESS

It's possible that after working for another company all your life you're eager to be on your own. If you don't want to stop working yet but you want to do things your way, consider starting a business. Becoming the CEO of your own company is easier today than it's ever been, particularly because many tasks can be done online from the comfort of your home. There's no need to acquire office space or inventory before you start your business.

Franchising is an extremely popular way to get into business for yourself. There are hundreds of franchises that are looking for operators in all states. These are ready-made businesses that are just waiting for an operator who can bring them to life. You pay an investment fee for the franchise tag. The parent company then provides the building, supplies, and training to get you up and running. The investment fee varies according to franchise, with more popular companies often requiring more investment. However, if you don't want to take years to get a company off the ground, franchising is the way to go. You'll even benefit from the franchise name for marketing purposes.

Another way to start a business is to become a consultant or freelancer. While drumming up business isn't as easy for consultants and freelancers as it is for franchisees, there are still thousands of opportunities available that would allow you to bring your expertise to the table and get paid for it. Platforms like Upwork, Freelancer, and Fiverr are some of the best places to find people who need your skills. You'll submit a bid to jobs you like, make yourself sound as attractive as possible (both in terms of what you can do and how much you charge), and start landing paying jobs. You may need to start with small jobs to build your reputation, but soon you'll have a thriving business of your own.

53

SHADOW SOMEONE IN A CAREER YOU'VE ALWAYS ADMIRED

While this isn't a paying activity, career shadowing can provide a taste of a career you may have wanted to experience. For instance, you may not want to become a police officer or a firefighter at this stage in your life, but you can experience these roles by shadowing someone who already holds the job. Most police and fire departments will let you shadow their employees for free, but you'll have to contact them to arrange it. There are also very specific rules you'll have to follow to be allowed to shadow but getting to experience these exciting jobs is worth it.

Most other careers would likely welcome a shadow for a day as well. Companies often participate in "day on the job" activities for high school students, and there's no reason they wouldn't want to do the same thing for you just because you're older. Contact the public relations department of the company you're interested in shadowing to arrange a day to follow someone around. Just be aware that some companies may require you to sign non-disclosure agreements or safety waivers.

Another fun thing that does pay is to become an extra on a film set. Find out which movies or television shows are filming in your area and watch for open calls. Many times, you don't even need a professional portfolio to be cast as an extra, but it may help. There are also online casting boards available that will post extra jobs when they are looking for people, and those will let you know what you need to bring to be considered for the job. Headshots and union membership may be required for some jobs, so if you're interested in those, consult with a talent agency to get started.

54

LEAVE A LEGACY

Even though we may not want to think about it, we're all getting older, and there will be a day when we're not around anymore. Fortunately, if you plan ahead, you can leave a lasting legacy for generations to come, which will be much appreciated when your descendants want to learn about your life.

55

RECORD YOUR MEMORIES

You have many memories younger people will never know about unless you tell them, especially because things change so quickly now. Activities and items you grew up with have been all but forgotten except in movies and books from those days. Luckily, the same technology that has replaced many past processes and pastimes can help you preserve those memories forever.

The most common way to record memories is in book format, and writing (or typing) them can ensure you get the details just right. In this way, you can revise and edit your memories until they say exactly what you want them to. If you want to publish your book, you can even have it edited professionally to sell on Amazon or other websites. If you'd rather not formally write a book, just journaling your memories in a notebook is a wonderful way to leave them behind for your descendants. Plus, they'll have a record of your handwriting as well.

Recording your memories verbally has never been easier, either. If you have a smartphone, it can double as a voice recorder, so you can record thoughts whenever they come to you. The best part about recording your voice talking about memories is that your great-great grandchildren will have a piece of you even if you're not there with them. Your voice will carry on long after you've passed away, and there's nothing like hearing a story from the original source.

Another option to record your memories is hiring a biographer. You tell the stories, and the biographer records them in a way that's meaningful to you and your family members. Perhaps this would be on a website or in a book, but it could also be on a family video or presentation. You dictate how you want your story told and the biographer makes it happen.

56

CREATE YOUR FAMILY TREE

Genealogy has become extremely popular with people of all ages, but if no one in your family has taken the time to create your family tree, it might be an activity you want to undertake. Not only will you learn about relatives that helped make you who you are, but you'll also likely find people you didn't even know you were related to. Depending on how far back you can trace your family, you might just discover you're descended from royalty!

Creating your family tree also offers a wonderful opportunity to contact relatives you haven't spoken to in a while to get information about your ancestors. You might spark memories and stories you've never heard, helping you learn more about your bloodline. Maybe you'll learn you got your sense of humor from a great, great uncle on your dad's side or that your hot temper has been in your family for generations. We can always learn more about ourselves and looking to our past is a great way to do it.

If you're adopted, this might seem like an activity to skip; however, with the online DNA databases available today, you could discover relatives that, until this technology was developed, would have remained unknown. Certainly, not every adopted person will be able to find their family this way, and not everyone wants to, but it is an option for you if you're intrigued about your ancestors. You could also potentially learn about any health conditions to which you're predisposed as well.

57

ESTABLISH A TRADITION WITH YOUR GRANDCHILDREN

When you think back on your life, some of your best memories are likely with grandparents. Often, grandparents seem magical to young children because they can do things perhaps children can't do with their parents. The times children spend with their grandparents are usually special because they don't get to see them every day, like they do immediate family. If you have grandchildren, take advantage of these relationships and establish a tradition or two with the little ones in your life.

Many traditions with grandparents revolve around holidays. For instance, you could create the tradition of baking cookies for Christmas with your grandchildren to give to neighbors and friends. Or you could take them Christmas caroling on the first Saturday of December. For Halloween, you might be the one to take them trick-or-treating, or perhaps you could have them over the

Friday before Halloween to watch spooky (age-appropriate) movies and have popcorn. Whatever you decide to do, start when they're small and keep up with it as they grow. They'll have wonderful memories of this time with you and will likely pass them on to their own children.

If you don't want to create traditions around holidays, you can always establish them in after school times or on special grandparent days. The key to making these traditions stick with your grandkids is to either make them routine (on a daily, weekly, or monthly basis) or make them extremely special so they stand out among their memories, even when they're young. Of course, as long as you're in their lives, their memories of you will be important to them, but having a tradition will help you leave an even stronger impression.

58

CREATE A SCRAPBOOK OF YOUR LIFE

Another fun way to record your memories is to create a scrapbook of your life. Not only are you writing down memories, you're also including artifacts like photographs and memorabilia to go with them. This is a nice way to showcase the important events in your life, and if you've saved souvenirs, you can create a visual memory of special times for future generations. For instance, remember that awesome concert you went to when you were 16? You probably even saved the ticket stubs or posters from that night. You can create a scrapbook page of the pictures, tickets, and poster to give someone an idea of what that experience was like. Don't forget to record your own memories of those events as well!

If you're looking for a meaningful gift to give the loved ones in your life, consider making a scrapbook that highlights your relationship with each one. Include photos of you and that person together, along with any souvenirs from the times you've spent with each other.

These scrapbooks will be personally sentimental for the recipients, and they're likely to keep them for the rest of their lives and may even pass them to their children, making them a family heirloom for generations to come.

Scrapbooks aren't the only way to provide a personalized gift to the people you love. Photo albums, letters, and other handmade presents that center on your relationship with the other person will be cherished for a lifetime and will provide a lasting legacy long after your years on Earth are over. Take the time now to cement your mark on your family through scrapbooks and other memory preservation processes so you have no regrets in your later years.

59

ADD SPICE

Now for the fun part! What makes being 60 years old great is that you have done what you're supposed to do for years and now you can do what you want. Certainly, as we've shown above, there are plenty of things you still should do, and there are many fun suggestions as well. However, now's the time for you to try some things you've never done before and add some spice to your life.

60

DATE FOR FUN

If you're a single senior, you may be hesitant to get back into dating, especially when you remember how difficult it was when you were younger. Surprisingly, it can be a lot of fun to go on dates when you're older, particularly if you have the mindset that you're doing it only for fun. There is no need to look for a long-term commitment unless that's what you really want. You can date people just for the social aspect and not worry about where the relationship will go from there.

As you may know, given the numerous television and social media ads, there are several forums for seniors looking to date. You can try a dating service or an online dating platform designed for older people. Be sure to put on your profile that you're not looking for a long-term commitment or that you're only dating for friendship purposes. This will help narrow the people with whom you're matched or who can contact you. The best part about dating when you're older is that you already know what you like in a person and what you don't. You'll probably be better able to spot people who you'll want in your life and those who you'll only see once, and you won't agonize over your decisions like you might have done when you were younger.

Try dating multiple people to expand your social life and surround yourself with additional support as you get older. You can never have too many friends, and dating is a wonderful way of finding more people with whom to do things and to introduce you to new activities. Just be clear up front what you're looking for to avoid setting unrealistic expectations with anyone you're dating, and you'll probably have a really good time.

61

LOOK UP A
FORMER FLAME

You might not be into dating apps or match-making services, but you may be interested in rekindling an old flame. With social media as prevalent as it is, you can probably find an old boyfriend or girlfriend fairly easily. In fact, you may already be in contact with them through Facebook, Twitter, or Instagram. If you're both single, there's nothing keeping you from seeing if that flame still burns. Take a chance and ask to go on a date with them to find out!

Even if you're not single, it might still be interesting to look up a former flame just to reminisce. Just as going through the process of creating a scrapbook can bring back memories that have long been buried, chatting with someone you spent a lot of time with when you were younger can have the same effect. It's good for us to remember the great times (and not-so-great times) to appreciate how far we've come and how much our lives have changed.

You can also do the same thing with long-lost friends instead of former flames, if you prefer not to open that can of worms. Try to find people you were friends with once but who have drifted away in recent years. Start with social media, and if you can't find them on one of the major platforms, reach out to mutual friends to see if you can get a mailing or email address to contact them. Even if you no longer connect the way you once did, it's still fun to talk about memories.

Remember that looking up a former friend or flame doesn't have to translate into a future relationship. Even if you just talk one or two times, the memories these conversations can invoke can be uplifting for both of you. Reconnecting with old friends is a way to keep your past alive and enrich your current life.

62

SPEAK YOUR MIND

For most of your life, you might have had to hold your tongue when you really wanted to state your opinion. Whether it was because you were afraid of losing your job or offending the wrong person, you may have tempered your opinion to ensure peace. Now that you're older and possibly retired, there may be nothing standing in the way of letting others know how you really feel. There is a reason we tend to become more outspoken as we get older, and it's because we tend to feel like we no longer have anything to lose.

Not only that, we also tend to become more confident in our beliefs, so we're more likely to let others know our opinion because we can better support it. We have lifelong experiences that have shaped our beliefs, and we can use those experiences to back up our opinions in the face of a challenge. With maturity also comes the ability to state our opinions in a way that is often better received than when we're younger. In other words, we often have more tact than people who are just learning how to diplomatically state their opinions.

In today's politically charged climate, you may still be hesitant to take a stand, but if not now, when? Giving your opinion about controversial topics will solidify who you are, which will help tell your story to future generations. If you really want to make your mark on the world, people have to know who you are, and part of that knowledge is understanding your values and beliefs. Speaking your mind might add a little drama to your life, but there's nothing wrong with having interesting conversations in which not everyone agrees.

63

TAKE RISKS

While you might be taking a risk by speaking your mind, there are other risks you may consider now that you're 60 years old. For instance, if you've always wanted to write a book but have been afraid of rejection, maybe now is the right time to submit your writing to a publisher and take that risk. You never know what will happen. Maybe your book is a best-seller waiting to happen and you would never know it if you didn't turn it in.

The same is true for other things you might have put off because you were afraid of the results. Maybe you've always wanted to act in a play but have been nervous about auditioning. Or perhaps you have an invention you know could change the world, but you've never researched how to get it produced and on the market. This is your chance to do something amazing, and maybe your last one.

The risks you take don't have to be huge risks, either. Maybe you just apply for a grant or scholarship to go back to school and earn your degree. This is a risk, especially if money is what has been preventing you from more education. Even just singing karaoke at your favorite bar can be a risk if you've never done it before. However, you might find you have a lot of fun and it could become your new hobby! If you never take the risk, you'll never know.

Certainly, the fear of rejection might still be getting in your way of any of these risks. No one likes getting rejected, so learning to deal with that possibility is the way to remove that fear. There are many approaches to getting over the fear of rejection. Research how to prepare yourself for it before you take the plunge. This will help you learn how to deal with the possibility of rejection so you can take even more risks. Keep in mind that the upside of taking the risk is usually far greater than the downside of rejection.

64

DO SOMETHING OUTSIDE YOUR COMFORT ZONE

Along with taking risks, doing things outside your comfort zone can add excitement to your life. Just because you're getting older doesn't mean you need to play it safe when it comes to what you do for entertainment. When you think about the things you've already done in your life, do you have any regrets? If so, now may be the time to take care of that so those regrets are no longer lingering in the back of your mind. Of course, there are some things you may never be able to do, such as becoming a professional football player or flying a jet plane in the middle of combat, but there are many other things you can still do to fulfill your dreams.

Bungee jumping, skydiving, scuba diving, parasailing, treasure hunting, ziplining, and other adventurous activities are all available to you now, just as they were when you were younger. Don't let your age prevent you from partaking in these activities. They all require instruction, whether you're 20 or 60 years old, so the only thing stopping you from doing these things is you. Even if you're scared to jump off a bridge or out of an airplane, overcoming your fear and doing it will be one of the most exhilarating moments of your life.

However, these adventurous activities aren't the only way you can do something outside your comfort zone. You can explore your wild side by taking smaller risks like visiting a topless beach or going skinny dipping for the first time. These are activities you might have been a little nervous about trying but have always wanted to do. Take the chance and do them because with every day that passes, the likelihood becomes greater you will miss out on these experiences.

65

SET A GUINNESS WORLD RECORD

Wouldn't it be cool to see your name on a world record? Even if your world record is broken at some point in the future, your name will always be in the record books for the year you set it. This is a wonderful way to leave your mark on the world and is something your family will talk about for generations to come. When you read the Guinness Book of World Records, you will discover there are records for just about anything and everything, including things that don't take much effort at all.

When we think of world records, we often conjure up images of Olympic athletes who accomplish feats no normal person could ever equal. However, there are records anyone can attempt, and many of them are beaten by people with no special training. For instance, some of the easier world records you could attempt include creating the tallest toilet paper tower in 30 seconds, being the fastest to arrange the alphabet from a can of alphabet soup, having the longest-lasting group hug, or cracking the most eggs with one hand in one minute.

To officially break a world record and be listed in the Guinness Book of World Records, you have to follow a specific procedure that includes registering for an account and applying for the record you want to break. You will also have to submit evidence of the broken record to allow Guinness to assess your effort. Evidence may include video proof, witnesses, a log book, or other documents. If your attempt requires more evidence, the review panel will let you know what else they need to certify the record.

There is also a cost for applying to break an existing world record, which currently is $800. If you apply to break a record that doesn't yet exist, the cost is even higher. For this reason, you may want to gather a few friends to attempt a world record instead of trying to do it yourself so you can split the cost among you. However, $800 really isn't that much when it comes to having your name in the record books for all time, so if you want to break an individual record, go for it!

66

GET A TATTOO

Believe it or not, tattoos are not just for young people. These days, everyone is getting a tattoo, so if you have a meaningful design you'd like to preserve on your skin forever, don't let misconceptions about tattoos stop you. As long as you get your tattoo from a legitimate shop that follows required hygienic standards, getting a tattoo is a perfectly safe way to uniquely display artwork.

As you know, a tattoo is (basically) forever, so make sure the design you pick is one you're comfortable having on your skin for the rest of your life. There are tattoo removal options, but they are often uncomfortable and take a long time to work, so you should consider a tattoo permanent. Luckily, by the time you're 60, if you've ever thought about having a tattoo in the past, you probably already know what you want or at least have an idea of a design you'd love for a lifetime.

Before you get a tattoo, ask for artist recommendations from your friends or research local artists yourself.

Choose one who can create the exact design you have in mind or who has a ready-made template you really want. Consider starting with a small tattoo on your ankle or shoulder, either of which can easily be covered up with clothing in situations where you don't want it to show. Just be aware that getting tattoos can be addictive, so once you get your first one, you might start thinking about your next design!

CONCLUSION

Turning 60 years old is a milestone that should be celebrated in a million different ways. These 60 things to do when turning 60 should get you started on the life you want as you look ahead to your golden years. Now is the beginning of the rest of your life, so take advantage of the opportunity and enjoy the ride!

Made in United States
Orlando, FL
27 October 2022